Drawing with Shapes Is Fun!

DRAWING A FISH WITH TRIANGLES

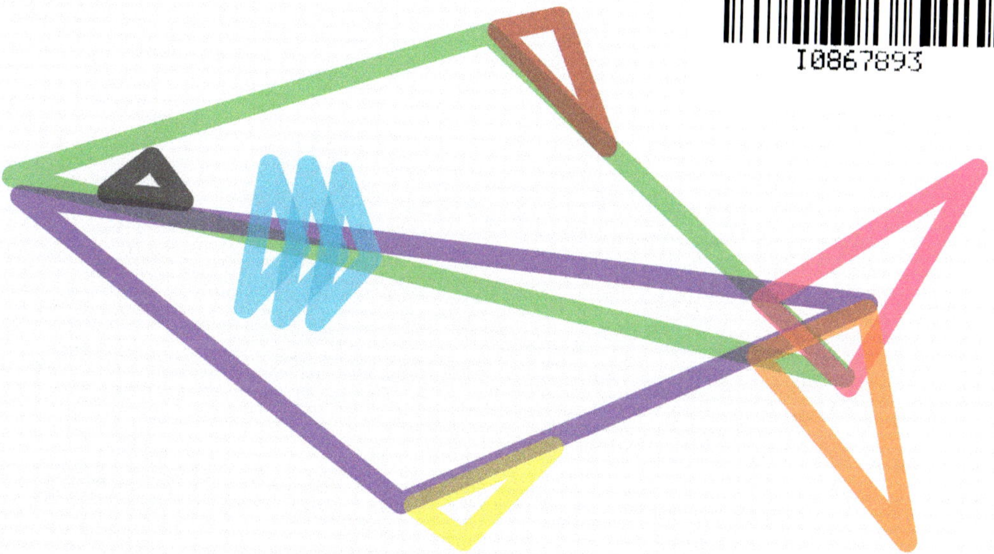

Sara Milner

PowerKiDS press.
New York

Published in 2019 by The Rosen Publishing Group, Inc.
29 East 21st Street, New York, NY 10010

First Edition

Editor: Greg Roza
Book Design: Reann Nye

Photo Credits: Cover, pp. 1–22 (background) piotr_pabijan/Shutterstock.com; cover, pp. 1–22 (markers) Photo Melon/Shutterstock.com; pp. 5, 24 Serg_dibrova/Shutterstock.com.

Cataloging-in-Publication Data

Names: Milner, Sara.
Title: Drawing a fish with triangles / Sara Milner.
Description: New York : PowerKids Press, 2019. | Series: Drawing with shapes is fun! | Includes index.
Identifiers: LCCN ISBN 9781538331088 (pbk.) | ISBN 9781538331071 (library bound) | ISBN 9781538331095 (6 pack)
Subjects: LCSH: Fishes in art–Juvenile literature. | Drawing–Technique–Juvenile literature. | Triangle in art–Juvenile literature.
Classification: LCC NC781.M53 2019 | DDC 743.6'7-dc23

Manufactured in the United States of America

CPSIA Compliance Information: Batch #CS18PK: For Further Information contact Rosen Publishing, New York, New York at 1-800-237-9932

CONTENTS

Fish live in water. They can have many colors. Let's draw a fish!

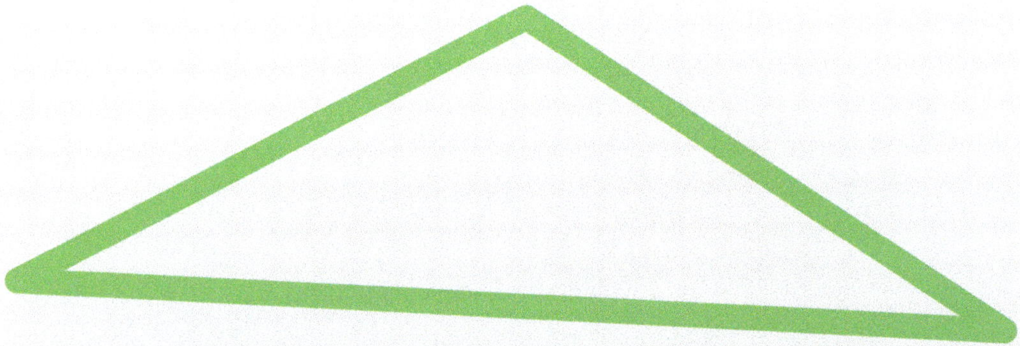

Draw a green triangle for the top of your fish.

Draw a purple triangle for the body of your fish.

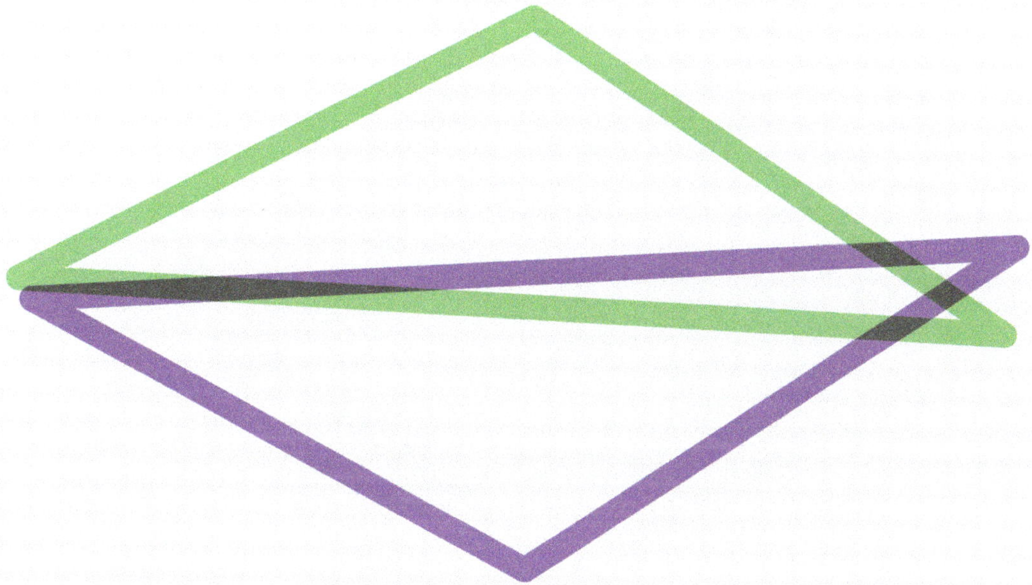

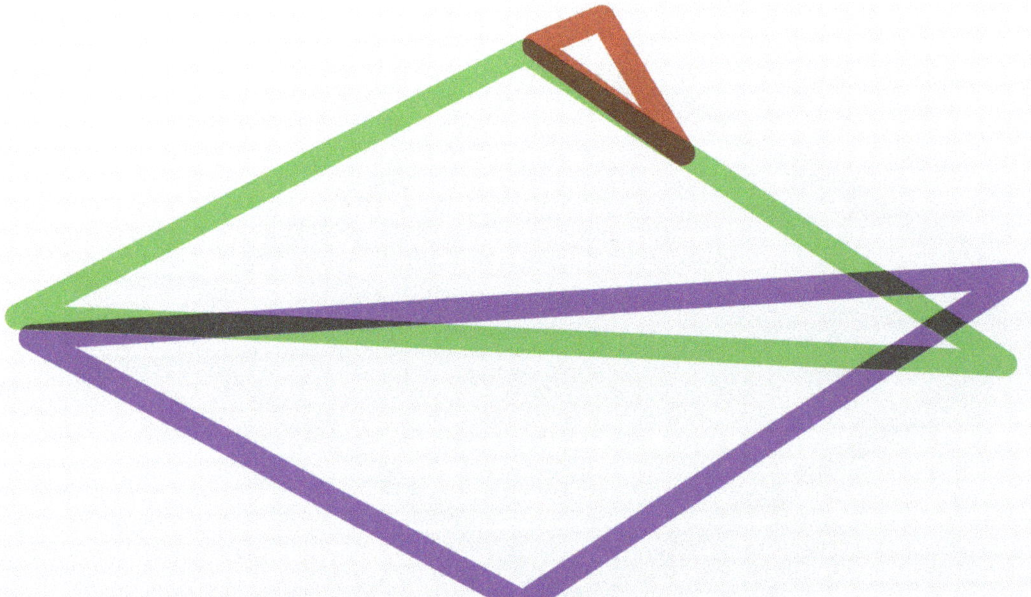

Draw a red triangle for a **fin** on top of your fish.

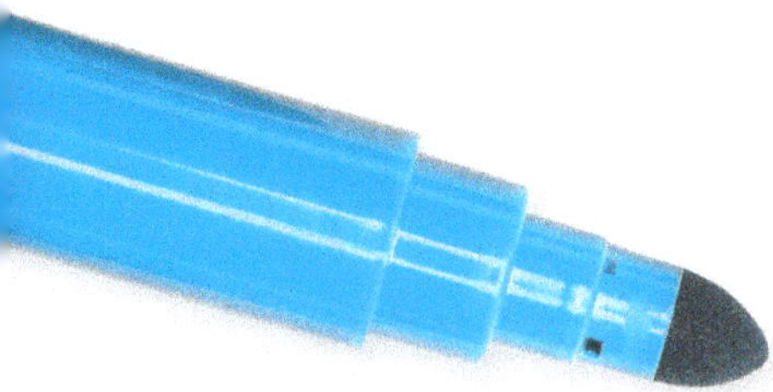

Draw three small blue triangles on the body of your fish.

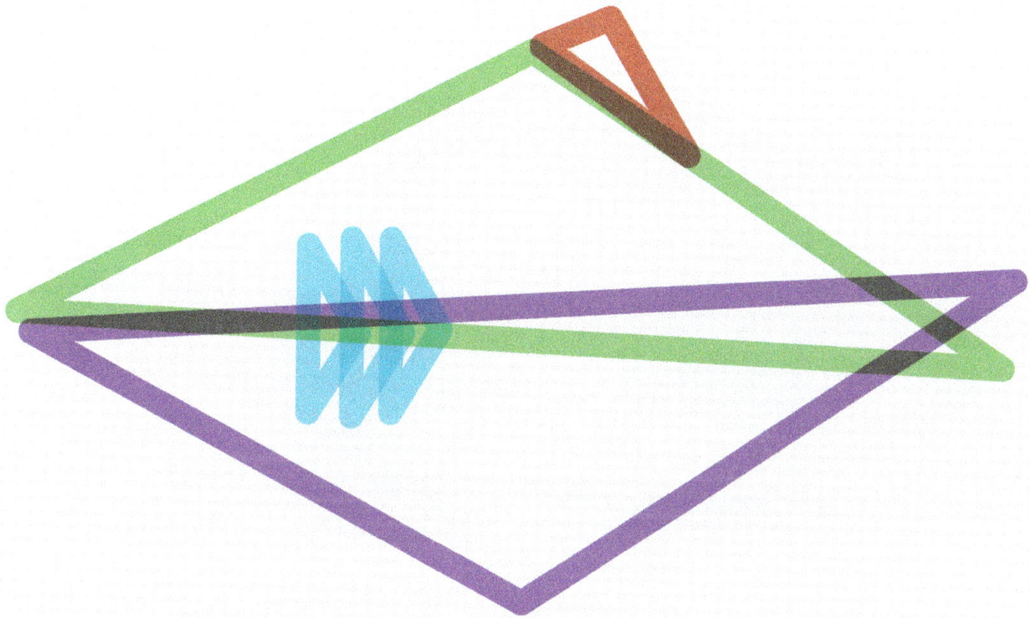

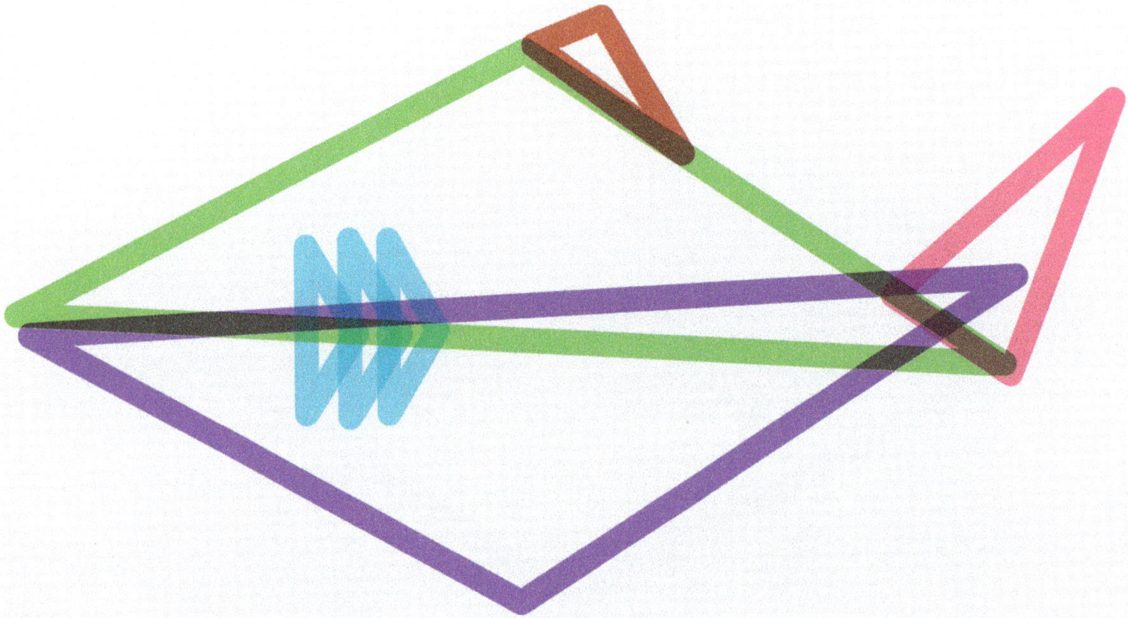

Draw a pink triangle for the top of the **tail**.

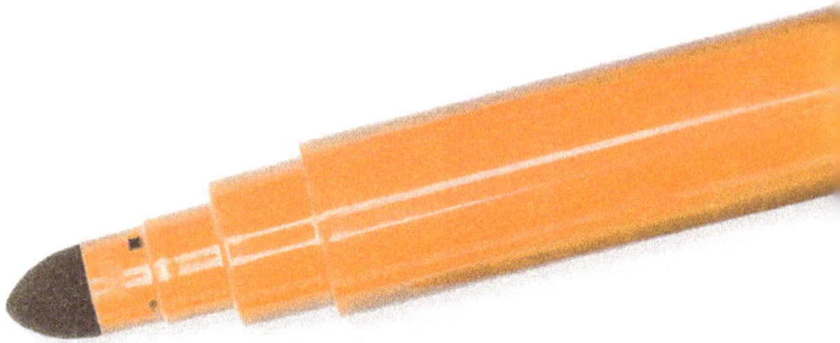

Draw an orange triangle for the tail of your fish.

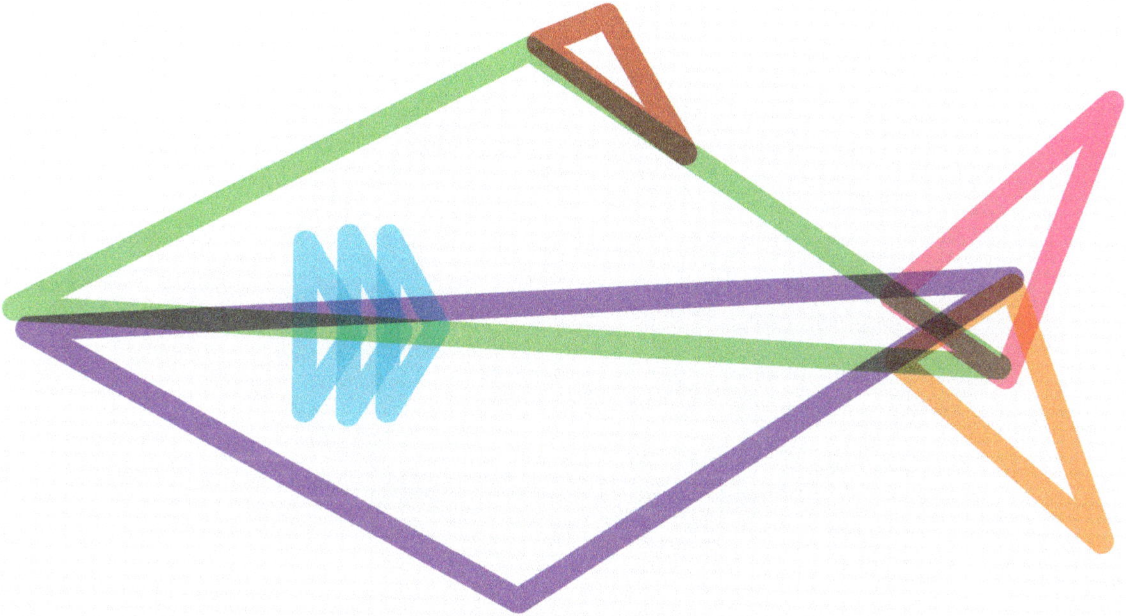

Draw a yellow triangle for a fin on the body of your fish.

Draw a small black triangle for the **eye** of your fish.

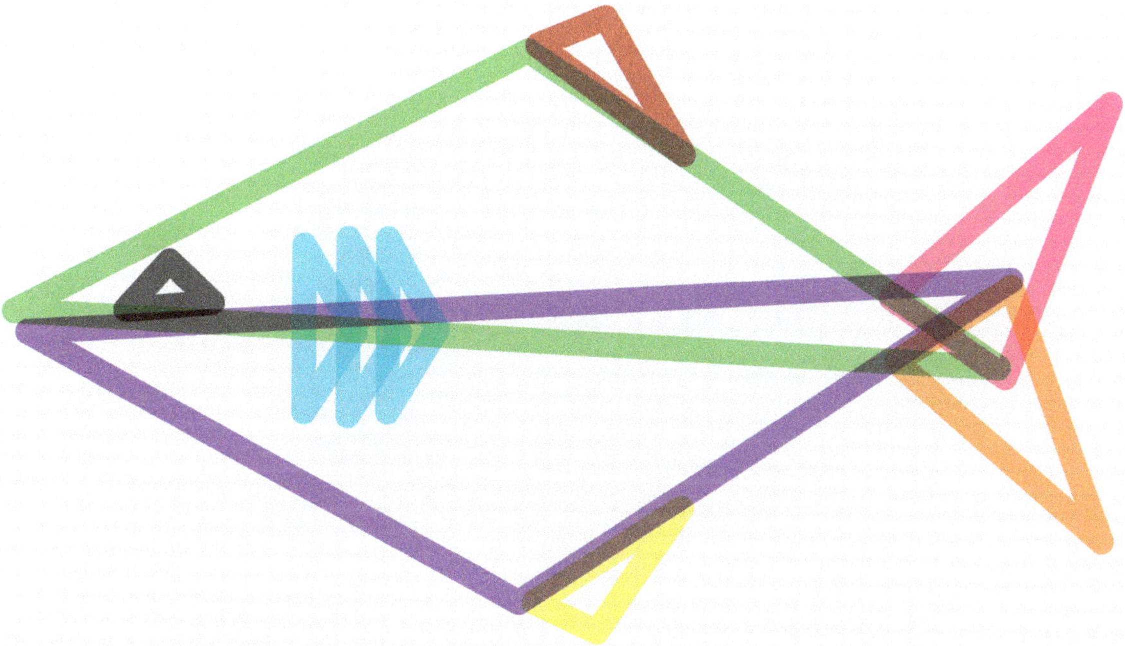

Color in your fish. Nice work!

WORDS TO KNOW

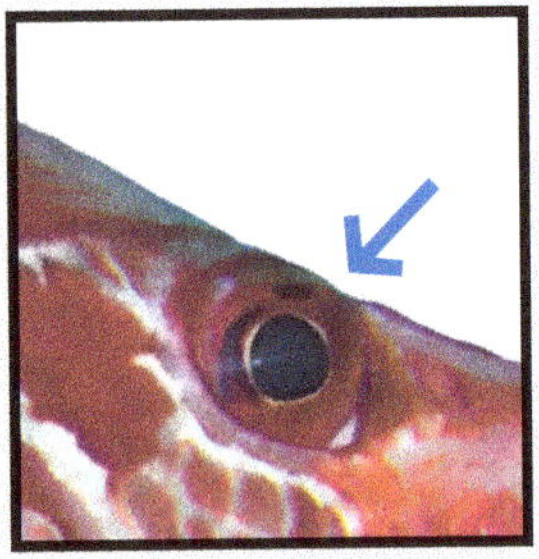

eye

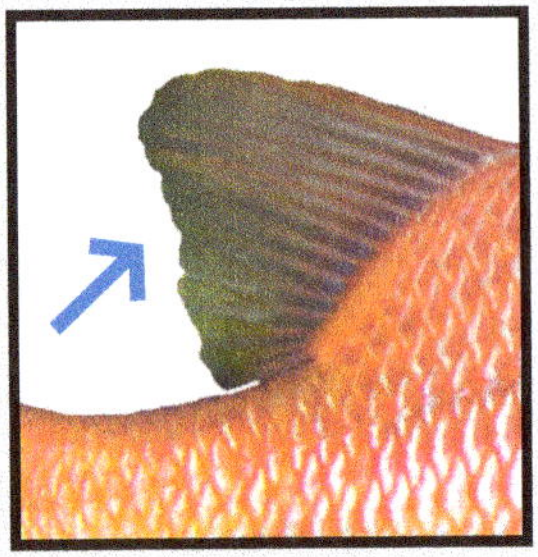

fin

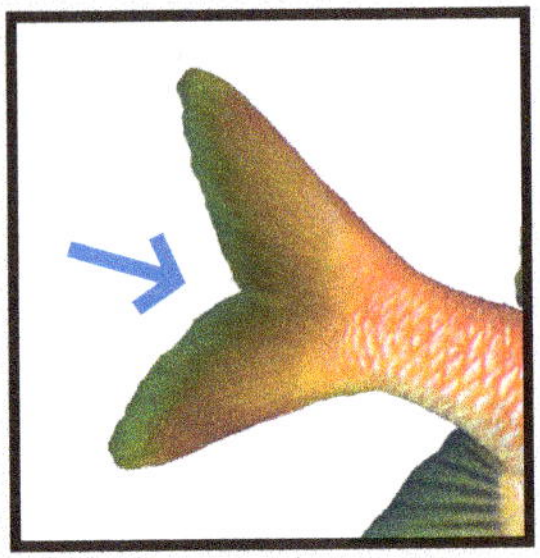

tail

INDEX

WEBSITES

Due to the changing nature of Internet links, PowerKids Press has developed an online list of websites related to the subject of this book. This site is updated regularly. Please use this link to access the list: www.powerkidslinks.com/dws/fish